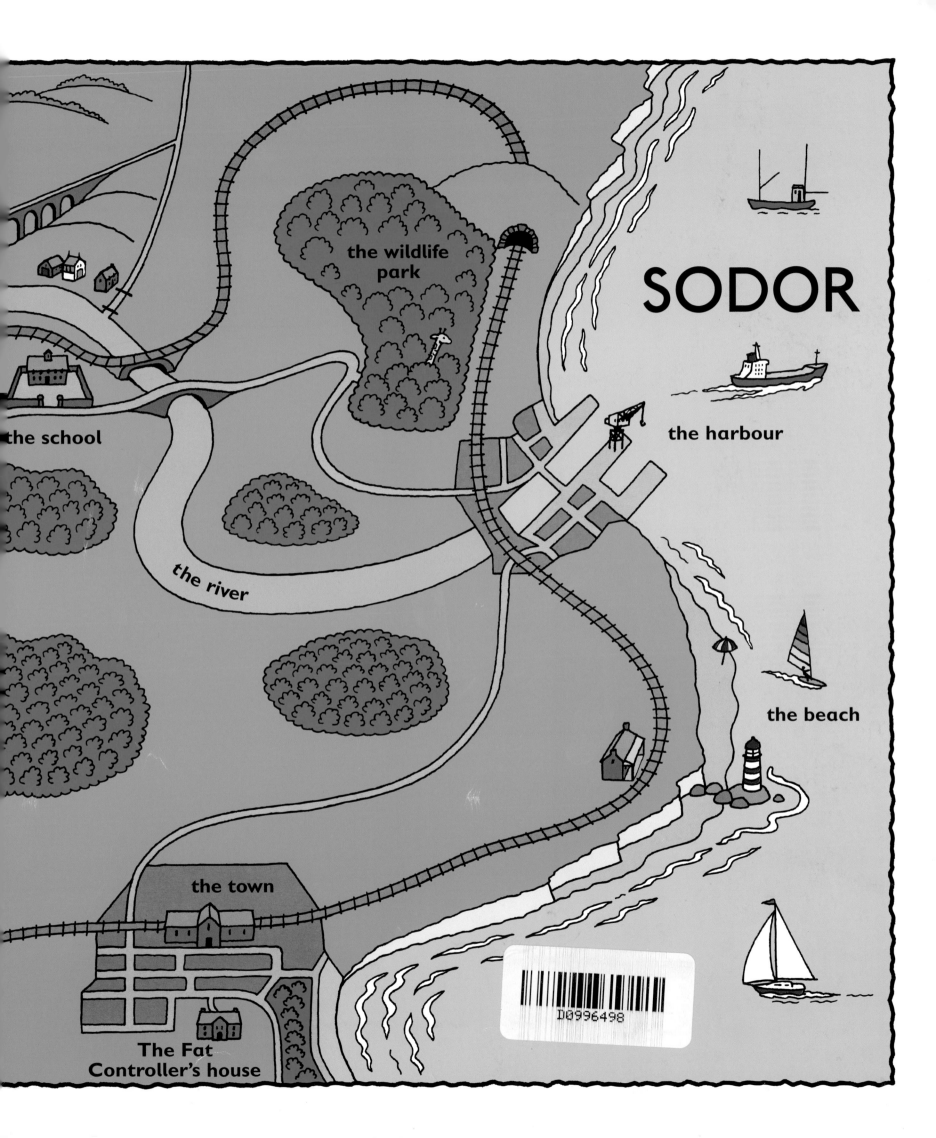

First published in 1999 by Egmont Books Limited

Published in this edition in 2004 by Dean, an imprint of Egmont Books Limited,
239 Kensington High Street, London W8 6SA

Thomas the Tank Engine & Friends

A BRITT ALLCROFT COMPANY PRODUCTION

Based on The Railway Series by The Rev W Awdry

© Gullane (Thomas) LLC 2004

ISBN 0 603 56160 8

Printed and bound in Singapore

THOMAS'
Really Useful
WORD BOOK

Based on The Railway Series by The Rev. W. Awdry

AT THE STATION

water tower

Duck

coal bunker

Edward

siding

trucks

turntable

points

roof

Toby

signal

buffers

signal box

James

rails

Annie

Clarabel

Annie

BOBO

road

red bag

teddy bear

pink bucket and spade

suitcase

litter bin

• ON THE PLATFORM •

buffet

Snacks/Drinks

OPEN

newspaper kiosk

bench

station master

parcels

FRAGILE

buggy

coal

driver

white line

guard

platform

The Fat Controller

porter

waiting room

clock

ticket office

TO PLATFORMS
2, 3 and **4**

passenger

carriage

Annie

trunk

luggage
trolley

family

brown briefcase

green flag

yellow umbrella

blue parcel

pigeon

IN THE COUNTRY

piglet

thrush

lamb

bull

cockerel

ON THE FARM

Terence

farmhouse

pigsty

stable

cat

milk
churn

boots

ax

farmer

horse

straw
bale

goat

cattle grid

hedgehog

haystack

barn

ewe   ram

hen house

barrel

log

chicken

farm truck   pond

ducks

Trevor

calf

cows

robin

sheepdog

donkey

chicks

sparrow

BY THE RIVER

aqueduct

sail

Bulstrode

river bank

yacht

dinghy

BULSTRODE

fender

police boat

POLICE

school

children

playground

wall

hamster

crayons

dinosaur

pirate hat

Thomas book

AT SCHOOL

blackboard

globe

paint brushes

paintings

Spring

computer

teacher

chalk

register

books

desk

drum

toy car

fish tank

tambourine

fish food

recorder

Summer   Autumn   Winter

play house

window

doll

cupboard

blocks

jigsaw

train set

table

chair

mask   crown   cowboy hat   dressing-up box

aeroplane

pen

jigsaw piece

goldfish

apple

IN THE WILDLIFE PARK

buffalo

polar bear

penguin

kangaroo

elephant

hippopotamus

flamingo

tiger

rhinoceros

Wildlife Park

Bertie

camel

ticket office

school party

AT THE HARBOUR

crab

capstan winch

dolphin

mop

flatfish

beach

crane

buoy

container

ladder

bow

container ship

diver

fish
market

fishing ne

rope

ferry

oil tanker

tug boat

lifeboat

stern

seagulls

jetty

mast

sailor

funnel

fork-lift truck

lobster pots

captain

harbour master

life belt

anchor

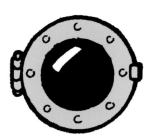

porthole

flag

lobster

sun

cliff

cafe

OPEN

ice cream van

steps

beach umbrella

puppet show

deck chair

sunhat

children

bucket

beach towel

sand castle

sunglasses

suntan lotion

spade

policeman

telephone box

motorbike

washing line

traffic lights

· IN THE TOWN ·

factory

park

playground

petrol station

carwash

statue

cinema

SQUINT & CO.

Mr. Bun

lorry

FOOT and

Annie

1

platform

steeple

house

town hall

driveway

church

fire engine

car

van

shops

coach

Dan D. Lion & Son

Eat CHEESE

street light

police car

road

TOYS B US

pavement

truck

petrol pump

aerial

door

swings

pair of glasses

BATHROOM

picture

chair

desk

tiles

taps

bath

shampoo

mirror

toilet

sink

BEDROOM

Harold

poster

blind

toy box

toys

letter box

front door

coat stand

mirror

telephone

floor tiles

vase

cushion

sofa

sideboard

carpet

vacuum cleaner

LIVING ROOM

I am 5

badge

party hat

bow

birthday present

pink shoes

THE BIRTHDAY PARTY

juggling balls

birthday cake

clown

plant pot

patio

unicycle

steps

dog

grass

flower bed

lemonade

fairy cakes

jelly

sausage rolls

glass

jug

biscuits

cheese

table cloth

presents

table

socks

children

bouncy castle

shoes

balloons

plates

bowls

party game

spoons

blanket

blue balloon

orange juice

crisps

candles

trumpet

the station

the farm